Punta Cana Travel Guide 2025

Beachfront Paradise In The Dominican Republic With Map & Images,Seaside Restaurants,lively Nightlife Scene,Adventurous Experiences

By

Arla J. Castillo

Disclaimer:

The information in this book is based on the author's research and experience. While every effort has been made to ensure the accuracy of the information, the author and publisher assume no responsibility for errors or omissions or for any consequences arising from the use of this material. Travelers are advised to verify details independently and take appropriate precautions.

Trademark Disclaimer

All product names, logos, brands, and trademarks mentioned in this book are the property of their respective owners. They are used for identification purposes only and do not imply endorsement, sponsorship, or affiliation with this book or its author.

The author and publisher acknowledge the rights of the trademark owners and have made every effort to attribute trademarks where applicable.

Table of Contents

Chapter 1.Introduction

Welcome to Punta Cana

As I got off the plane and felt the warm, humid air wash over me, I knew I was in for a wonderful surprise. Punta Cana, a bustling beachfront paradise in the Dominican Republic, had been calling my name for years, and I was finally here.

My first impression was one of wonder. The immaculate white sand beaches stretched as far as the eye could reach, lapped by crystal-clear turquoise waters. The sun shone brightly, putting a golden glow on all it touched. I couldn't resist the impulse to drop my clothing and dive right into the refreshing ocean.

My days in Punta Cana were filled with boundless sunlight, adventure, and leisure. I spent my mornings relaxing by the pool, sipping on tropical cocktails, and reading a nice novel. In the afternoons, I engaged in fascinating adventures, such as snorkeling through brilliant coral reefs, zip-lining through lush rainforests, and exploring undiscovered caves.

One of my favourite experiences was sailing on a catamaran to a quiet island. The crystal-clear seas were filled with marine life, and I had the opportunity to swim among colourful fish and lively dolphins. The island itself was a tropical haven, with swaying palm palms, smooth white beaches, and a superb seafood feast.

As the sun began to set, I would travel to one of the many seaside restaurants to experience the flavours of Dominican cuisine. The fresh seafood, tropical fruits, and vivid spices were a gourmet joy. I really appreciated the mofongo, a savoury meal made with mashed plantains, and the cool piña coladas.

At night, Punta Cana changed into a lively nightlife scene. I danced the night away in vibrant clubs, sipping on exotic cocktails and enjoying the infectious energy of the audience. The music, the people, and the ambiance were absolutely amazing.

Scan the QR code

1. Open Camera: Launch your smartphone's camera app.
2. Position QR Code: Place the QR code within the camera's viewfinder.
3. Hold Steady: Keep the device steady for the camera to focus.
4. Wait for Scan: Wait for the code to be recognized.
5. Tap Notification: Follow the prompt to access the content.

My journey to Punta Cana was more than simply a holiday; it was an escape to heaven. The magnificent beaches, adventurous experiences, great food, and colourful culture left an unforgettable impact on my heart. I can't wait to return to this tropical jewel and create more amazing experiences.

A quick summary of Punta Cana

Punta Cana, a sun-kissed paradise located at the easternmost tip of the Dominican Republic, has evolved as one of the most sought-after tourist destinations in the Caribbean. Renowned for its stunning white-sand beaches, crystal-clear turquoise waters, and world-class resorts, Punta Cana offers a perfect vacation for travellers seeking leisure, adventure, and cultural immersion.

With its gorgeous coastline reaching for miles, Punta Cana boasts some of the most spectacular beaches in the world. Bávaro Beach, in particular, is a favourite among travellers, with its beautiful sands and calm surf. The area also provides a wealth of water sports, from snorkelling and scuba diving to surfing and kiteboarding, catering to thrill-seekers and water enthusiasts alike.

Beyond its natural beauty, Punta Cana offers a dynamic cultural experience. Visitors can immerse themselves in the Dominican Republic's rich history and traditions, explore attractive rural communities, and sample exquisite local food. The area is also home to a range of luxury resorts and all-inclusive complexes, ensuring a pleasant and unforgettable visit.

Whether you're looking for a romantic getaway, a family holiday, or an adventure-filled excursion, Punta Cana has something to offer everyone. Its gorgeous beaches, crystal-clear oceans, and vibrant culture make it a genuinely unique trip.

Why visit Punta Cana

Here are some strong reasons to visit Punta Cana:

Pure Beaches: Punta Cana features miles of pure, white-sand beaches lapped by crystal-clear turquoise waters. It's a paradise for sunbathers, swimmers, and water sports aficionados.

All-Inclusive Luxury: The area is famed for its all-inclusive resorts, offering top-notch amenities, exquisite cuisine, and unending entertainment. You may relax, refresh, and indulge without any worries.

Thrilling Water activities: From snorkelling and scuba diving to surfing and kiteboarding, Punta Cana provides a wealth of water activities for adventure lovers. Explore beautiful coral reefs, encounter aquatic life, or catch some waves.

Cultural Experiences: Immerse yourself in the rich Dominican culture by visiting local towns, trying traditional cuisine, and learning about the country's history.

Ideal temperature: Punta Cana boasts a warm, tropical temperature year-round, making it an ideal place for a winter vacation or a summer getaway.

Family-Friendly Fun: With its safe beaches, water parks, and kid-friendly activities, Punta Cana is a perfect choice for a family vacation.
Romantic Escapes: Couples may enjoy secluded beaches, romantic dinners, and exquisite spa treatments in Punta Cana.

Affordable Luxury: Compared to other Caribbean locations, Punta Cana offers outstanding value for money, making it accessible to a wide variety of guests.

Whether you're seeking relaxation, action, or a combination of all, Punta Cana offers something to offer everyone. It's a tropical paradise that guarantees amazing moments.

The best time to visit

The greatest time to visit Punta Cana is during the dry season, which spans from December to April. During these months, you might expect:

Pleasant Weather: Warm, sunny days with low rainfall.

Lower Humidity:More comfortable circumstances for outdoor activities.

Peak Season: This is the busiest time of year, so expect higher prices and greater crowds.

Shoulder Seasons (May and November):
These months offer an excellent balance between favourable weather and fewer tourists. While there may be rare rain showers, they are normally short-lived. Prices for lodgings and activities are frequently more reasonable during these months.

Rainy Season (June to October):
While the rainy season brings more humidity and occasional showers, it's still possible to spend a nice holiday in Punta Cana. The lush flora is at its height, and there are fewer visitors. However, be prepared for potential rain delays and greater humidity levels.

The best time to visit Punta Cana depends on your unique choices and priorities. If you prefer excellent weather and don't mind the crowds, the dry season is the ideal time to go. If you want fewer crowds and cheaper pricing, the shoulder seasons are an excellent option. And if you're daring and don't mind the rain, the rainy season can offer unique experiences.

Chapter 2. Planning Your Trip

How to get to Punta Cana

Pre-booked Private Transfer

A pre-booked private transfer is a simple and hassle-free method to get from the Punta Cana International Airport to your accommodation. A professional driver will be waiting for you at the airport, ready to transport you directly to your destination.
Cost: Prices vary depending on the distance and vehicle size, but normally range from $25 to USD 100 per car, one-way.

Shared Shuttle
Shared shuttles are a budget-friendly option for going from Punta Cana International Airport to famous tourist spots like Bávaro and Punta Cana. They normally operate on a defined route, stopping at several hotels along the way.

Routes:

- Punta Cana International Airport to Bávaro

- Punta Cana International Airport to Punta Cana

Terminals:

Departure: Punta Cana International Airport

Arrival: Various hotels in Bávaro and Punta Cana

Cost:

Approximately $15-USD 25 per person, one-way.

Taxi

Taxis are readily available at the Punta Cana International Airport. They may drive you to numerous sites within Punta Cana, including Bávaro, Cabeza de Toro, and other major tourist areas.

Routes:

- Punta Cana International Airport to Bávaro

- Punta Cana International Airport to Punta Cana

- Punta Cana International Airport to Cabeza de Toro

Terminals:

Departure: Punta Cana International Airport

Arrival: Your precise destination inside Punta Cana

Cost:
Taxi fares are not metered, thus it's vital to discuss the amount with the driver beforehand. The cost can vary based on the route and traffic circumstances but anticipate paying roughly $30-$100 USD for a one-way ride.

Rental Car

Renting a car in Punta Cana offers the utmost flexibility to explore the island at your speed. You can quickly move between different beaches, attractions, and towns.

Routes:

Punta Cana International Airport to Bávaro: A popular route for beachgoers and resort-hoppers.

Punta Cana International Airport to Punta Cana: This route takes you to the main town area, where you can find stores, restaurants, and nightlife.

Punta Cana International Airport to Macao Beach: This path goes to a wonderful, less populated beach with big waves, great for surfing.

Terminals:

Departure: Punta Cana International Airport

Arrival: Your chosen destination inside Punta Cana

Cost:
Automobile rental fees vary depending on the rental business, automobile type, and rental term. On average, anticipate to pay roughly $30-USD 50 every day.

Visa requirements

Visa Requirements for Punta Cana
For most countries, including US, Canadian, and European nationals, a visa is not required for stays of up to 30 days. However, you will require a valid passport and a completed electronic immigration/customs form (E-Ticket) which can be filled out online before your arrival.

It's vital to check the particular visa requirements for your nationality closer to your departure date, as immigration laws sometimes change. You can contact the Dominican Republic's official tourism website or your local embassy for the most up-to-date information.

Currency and exchange rates

Currency & Exchange Rates in Punta Cana
The official currency of the Dominican Republic is the Dominican Peso (DOP). While you can convert currencies at the airport or banks, it's typically more convenient to utilise US dollars. Many shops, especially in tourist locations like Punta Cana, take US money.

Exchange Rates:

US Dollar to Dominican Peso: The conversion rate changes, but generally, you can expect to acquire roughly 50-60 Dominican Pesos for 1 US Dollar.

Euro to Dominican Peso: The conversion rate for Euros to Dominican Pesos also changes.

Tips for Currency Exchange:

Airport Exchange: While convenient, airport exchange rates can be less attractive. Consider exchanging a modest amount for emergency requirements and swap larger quantities at banks or exchange houses in town.

ATMs: ATMs are readily available in Punta Cana and give reasonable exchange rates. However, be mindful of potential costs paid by your bank.

Credit Cards: Major credit cards are accepted at many hotels, restaurants, and businesses. However, it's always a good idea to have some cash on hand for little purchases and tips.

Additional Tips:

Negotiate: In local markets and with street sellers, it's normal to negotiate pricing. Don't be scared to haggle for a better offer.

Tipping: Tipping is usual in Punta Cana, especially for services like restaurant waiters, bellhops, and tour guides. A tip of 10-15% is often regarded as appropriate.

Accommodation options

Luxury Hotels

Zoetry Agua Punta Cana
Zoetry Agua Punta Cana is an all-inclusive luxury resort that offers an unsurpassed level of relaxation and renewal. Nestled amidst lush tropical gardens and exquisite white-sand beaches, this adults-only retreat provides a quiet getaway from the rush and bustle of everyday life.

Indulge in exquisite dining experiences at the resort's four à la carte restaurants, each offering a unique culinary journey. Sip on handcrafted cocktails at one of the three trendy bars or unwind with a refreshing spa treatment. The resort also has a state-of-the-art fitness facility, a yoga pavilion, and a range of water activities, guaranteeing that there's something for everyone.

Cost:

The cost of a stay at Zoetry Agua Punta Cana might vary according to the season and room choice. However, expect to pay roughly USD 367 each night for a double hotel.

How to Get There:

To reach Zoetry Agua Punta Cana, you can:

Pre-book a private transfer: A handy and hassle-free option, with fees ranging from $25 to USD 100 per vehicle, one-way.

Shared Shuttle: A more budget-friendly option, with rates of about $15-USD 25 per person, one-way.

Taxi: A flexible alternative, but be sure to discuss the fare beforehand. The cost might range from $30 to USD 100, depending on the distance.

Rental Car: Offers maximum flexibility to explore the area. Car rental fees vary but expect to pay roughly $30-USD 50 each day.

Sanctuary Cap Cana

Sanctuary Cap Cana is an elite adults-only resort tucked within the exclusive Cap Cana enclave. This magnificent resort offers a calm and refined escape, suitable for couples seeking tranquillity and enjoyment.

Immerse yourself in a world of luxury with spacious apartments, each with private plunge pools and spectacular ocean views. Relax on exquisite white-sand beaches, recuperate at the world-class spa, or tee off at the neighbouring Jack Nicklaus Signature Golf Course. The resort also boasts a choice of gourmet eating options, including beachfront restaurants and elegant bars.

Cost:
The cost of a stay at Sanctuary Cap Cana varies according to the season and accommodation type. However, expect to pay around USD 500 per night for a double hotel.

How to Get There:

To access Sanctuary Cap Cana, you can:

Pre-book a private transfer: A handy and hassle-free option, with fees ranging from $25 to USD 100 per vehicle, one-way.

Shared Shuttle: A more budget-friendly option, with rates of about $15-USD 25 per person, one-way.

Taxi: A flexible alternative, but be sure to discuss the fare beforehand. The cost might range from $30 to USD 100, depending on the distance.

Rental Car: Offers maximum flexibility to explore the area. Car rental fees vary but expect to pay roughly $30-USD 50 each day.

Eden Roc at Cap Cana
Eden Roc in Cap Cana is a magnificent boutique resort that offers a sophisticated and exclusive vacation. Nestled within the exclusive Cap Cana enclave, this Relais & Châteaux hotel mixes European grandeur with Caribbean charm.

Indulge in opulent accommodations, from spacious suites to private villas, each with its own private pool and magnificent ocean views. Relax by the infinity pool, recuperate at the world-class Solaya Spa, or eat delicious food at the resort's three gourmet restaurants.

Cost:
The cost of a stay at Eden Roc at Cap Cana varies depending on the season and room type. However, expect to pay around USD 800 per night for a double hotel.

How to Get There:

To access Eden Roc at Cap Cana, you can:
Pre-book a private transfer: A handy and hassle-free option, with fees ranging from $25 to USD 100 per vehicle, one-way.

Shared Shuttle: A more budget-friendly option, with rates of about $15-USD 25 per person, one-way.

Taxi: A flexible alternative, but be sure to discuss the fare beforehand. The cost might range from $30 to USD 100, depending on the distance.

Rental Car: Offers maximum flexibility to explore the area. Car rental fees vary but expect to pay roughly $30-USD 50 each day.

The Ritz-Carlton, Punta Cana
The Ritz-Carlton, Punta Cana, is a luxury beachfront resort that offers an unrivalled level of elegance and sophistication. This magnificent facility boasts spacious accommodations, world-class restaurants, and a wealth of recreational activities.

Indulge in a range of gourmet dining experiences at the resort's nine restaurants, each delivering a unique gastronomic adventure. Relax by the infinity pool, recuperate at the world-class spa, or tee off at the local golf course. The resort also has a state-of-the-art fitness centre, a kids' club, and a range of water activities.

Cost:
The cost of a stay at The Ritz-Carlton, Punta Cana might vary depending on the season and room type. However, expect to pay around USD 700 per night for a double hotel.

How to Get There:

To reach The Ritz-Carlton, Punta Cana, you can:

Pre-book a private transfer: A handy and hassle-free option, with fees ranging from $25 to USD 100 per vehicle, one-way.

Shared Shuttle: A more budget-friendly option, with rates of about $15-USD 25 per person, one-way.

Taxi: A flexible alternative, but be sure to discuss the fare beforehand. The cost might range from $30 to USD 100, depending on the distance.

Rental Car: Offers maximum flexibility to explore the area. Car rental fees vary but expect to pay roughly $30-USD 50 each day.

Budget-Friendly Hotels

Be Live Collection Punta Cana

Be Live Collection Punta Cana is a vibrant and active all-inclusive resort suitable for families and groups seeking fun and entertainment. This vast facility boasts a range of activities, including multiple pools, water slides, a casino, and a kids' club.

Enjoy wonderful food at the resort's buffet and à la carte restaurants, or sip on cool beverages at one of the many bars. The resort also offers a range of activities, such as beach volleyball, water aerobics, and live entertainment.

Cost:
The cost of a stay at Be Live Collection Punta Cana is fairly inexpensive, especially for families. Expect to pay roughly $200-USD 300 per night for a family room.

How to Get There:

To reach Be Live Collection Punta Cana, you can:
Pre-book a private transfer: A handy and hassle-free option, with fees ranging from $25 to USD 100 per vehicle, one-way.

Shared Shuttle: A more budget-friendly option, with rates of about $15-USD 25 per person, one-way.

Taxi: A flexible alternative, but be sure to discuss the fare beforehand. The cost might range from $30 to USD 100, depending on the distance.

Rental Car: Offers maximum flexibility to explore the area. Car rental fees vary but expect to pay roughly $30-USD 50 each day.

Grand Sirenis Punta Cana Resort

Grand Sirenis Punta Cana Resort is a luxury all-inclusive resort set between lush coconut orchards. It offers a wonderful blend of relaxation and excitement for families, couples, and groups of friends.

The resort features two gorgeous pools for adults, two separate pools for youngsters, and a water park with thrilling slides and attractions. You can also enjoy a range of water sports, including snorkelling, kayaking, and diving.

The resort's spacious rooms and suites are attractively constructed and equipped with modern facilities. You may indulge in great cuisine at the resort's nine restaurants, which provide a selection of international and local specialties.

Cost:

The cost of a stay at Grand Sirenis Punta Cana Resort varies depending on the season and room type. However, expect to pay roughly $300-USD 400 each night for family accommodation.

How to Get There:

To access Grand Sirenis Punta Cana Resort, you can:

Pre-book a private transfer: A handy and hassle-free option, with fees ranging from $25 to USD 100 per vehicle, one-way.

Shared Shuttle: A more budget-friendly option, with rates of about $15-USD 25 per person, one-way.

Taxi: A flexible alternative, but be sure to discuss the fare beforehand. The cost might range from $30 to USD 100, depending on the distance.

Rental Car: Offers maximum flexibility to explore the area. Car rental fees vary but expect to pay roughly $30-USD 50 each day.

Dreams Punta Cana Resort & Spa

Dreams Punta Cana Resort & Spa is an all-inclusive luxury resort located along a gorgeous, palm-studded beach in Uvero Alto. This AAA Four Diamond resort offers a wide selection of services and activities for guests of all ages.

One of the centrepieces of the resort is its large pool, which flows from the lobby down to the beach and contains a swim-up bar and different activities. Guests can also enjoy a range of water sports, such as snorkelling, kayaking, and diving, or relax on the gorgeous beach.

The resort offers a range of food options, including gourmet restaurants, a buffet, and 24-hour room service. For those seeking relaxation, the Dreams Spa provides a variety of pleasant services.

Cost:

The cost of a stay at Dreams Punta Cana Resort & Spa varies depending on the season and room type. However, expect to pay roughly $350-USD 450 each night for a family room.

How to Get There:

To access Dreams Punta Cana Resort & Spa, you can:

Pre-book a private transfer: A handy and hassle-free option, with fees ranging from $25 to USD 100 per vehicle, one-way.
Shared Shuttle: A more budget-friendly option, with rates of about $15-USD 25 per person, one-way.

Taxi: A flexible alternative, but be sure to discuss the fare beforehand. The cost might range from $30 to USD 100, depending on the distance.

Rental Car: Offers maximum flexibility to explore the area. Car rental fees vary but expect to pay roughly $30-USD 50 each day.

Barceló Bávaro Beach Resort

Barceló Bávaro Beach Resort is a magnificent all-inclusive resort suitable for adults seeking a fun-filled and restful holiday. This oceanfront facility offers a wide range of activities, including three pools, a casino, a spa, and a variety of water sports.

The resort's spacious rooms and suites are attractively constructed and equipped with modern facilities. You may indulge in great cuisine at the resort's nine restaurants, which provide a selection of international and local specialties.

One of the hallmarks of the resort is its lively atmosphere, with nightly entertainment, themed events, and live music. Whether you want to relax by the pool, dance the night away, or explore the local area, Barceló Bávaro Beach Resort provides something for everyone.

Cost:

The cost of a stay at Barceló Bávaro Beach Resort varies depending on the season and room type. However, expect to pay roughly $300-USD 400 per night for a double hotel.

How to Get There:

To access Barceló Bávaro Beach Resort, you can:

Pre-book a private transfer: A handy and hassle-free option, with fees ranging from $25 to $100 USD per vehicle, one-way.

Shared Shuttle: A more budget-friendly option, with rates of about $15-$25 USD per person, one-way.

Taxi: A flexible alternative, but be sure to discuss the fare beforehand. The cost might range from $30 to $100 USD, depending on the distance.

Rental Car: Offers maximum flexibility to explore the area. Car rental fees vary but expect to pay roughly $30-$50 USD each day.

Budgeting your trip

Budgeting Your Punta Cana Trip
Budgeting for a trip to Punta Cana might vary greatly based on your travel style, accommodations, and activities. Here's a broad breakdown to help you organise your expenses:

Accommodation

All-Inclusive Resorts: These are the most popular option in Punta Cana, offering a wide range of rates. Budget-friendly options start around $150 per night, while luxury resorts can cost upwards of $500 per night.

Hotels: Mid-range hotels normally cost between $100 and $200 per night, but budget hotels can be obtained for as low as $50 per night.

Vacation Rentals: Renting a villa or apartment can be a cost-effective choice, especially for bigger groups. Prices vary depending on the size and location of the property.

Transportation

Flights: Flight costs might vary greatly based on your departure location, travel dates, and airline. It's advisable to book your flights in advance and hunt for offers and specials.

Airport transports: You can select between shared shuttles, private transports, or taxis. Shared shuttles are the most budget-friendly alternative, while private transfers offer the most convenience.

Local Transportation: Renting a car provides the most flexibility to explore the island at your own speed. Taxis and public transportation are also available, however they may be less convenient.

Food and Drinks

All-Inclusive Resorts: Food and drinks are often included in the all-inclusive package.

Dining Out: Budget-friendly restaurants can be found for roughly $10 each meal, while mid-range restaurants can cost $20-$30 per meal.

Drinks: Local beers and cocktails are quite reasonable, although imported drinks can be more pricey.

Activities and Excursions

Water Sports: Many water sports, like snorkelling, kayaking, and paddleboarding, are commonly included in all-inclusive packages or can be leased at reasonable fees.

Excursions: Excursions like island hopping, deep-sea fishing, and zip-lining can vary in price, but they normally cost from $50 to $150 per person.

Additional Tips for Budgeting:

Travel During the Off-Season: Consider travelling during the off-season (May-November) to find reduced pricing on flights and lodgings.

Book in Advance: Booking your flights and accommodations in advance will help you acquire the best bargains.

Pack Light: Packing light will help you avoid baggage costs and make your trip experience more convenient.

Use a Travel Rewards Credit Card: Using a travel rewards credit card will help you earn points and miles that can be redeemed for future travel.

Consider All-Inclusive Resorts: All-inclusive resorts can be a wonderful way to budget your trip, as they generally include food, drinks, and activities in the price.

Chapter 3. Top Attractions and Activities

Shorelines

Beach Bávaro

Nestled in the middle of Punta Cana, Bávaro Beach is a world-class length of immaculate white sand and glistening blue sea. There are plenty of events this perfect paradise provides for guests of all ages.

Things to Do:

Sunbathing and swimming: Lay on the smooth beach, soak up the sun, then cool yourself in the warm Caribbean Sea.

Snorkel, scuba diving, kayaking, paddle boarding, and windsurfing among other water sports.

Join other guests in a casual beach volleyball game.

Beachfront bars and restaurants provide great local cuisine together with great beverages.
If you are lodging at a resort, use their facilities like fitness centres, spas, and swimming pools.

Cost:

The cost of enjoying Bávaro Beach depends on your chosen activities and accommodations.

Beach entry: Most beaches in Bávaro are free to enter.

Water Sports: Rental prices for water sports equipment normally vary from $20 to $50 per hour.

Resort Amenities: The cost of resort amenities varies depending on the specific resort and the services you choose.

Scan the QR code
1. Open Camera: Launch your smartphone's camera app.
2. Position QR Code: Place the QR code within the camera's viewfinder.
3. Hold Steady: Keep the device steady for the camera to focus.
4. Wait for Scan: Wait for the code to be recognized.
5. Tap Notification: Follow the prompt to access the content.

How to Get There:

To access Bávaro Beach, you can:
Pre-book a private transfer: A handy and hassle-free option, with fees ranging from $25 to USD 100 per vehicle, one-way.

Shared Shuttle: A more budget-friendly option, with rates of about $15-USD 25 per person, one-way.

Taxi: A flexible alternative, but be sure to discuss the fare beforehand. The cost might range from $30 to USD 100, depending on the distance.

Rental Car: Offers maximum flexibility to explore the area. Car rental fees vary but expect to pay roughly $30-USD 50 each day.

Punta Cana Beach
Punta Cana Beach is a gorgeous stretch of coastline that offers a wonderful blend of relaxation and action. With its silky white dunes, crystal-clear waters, and swaying palm trees, it's no wonder why it's a popular destination for tourists from around the world.

Things to Do:
Sunbathing and Swimming: Relax on the gorgeous shores, soak up the sun, and take a refreshing plunge in the warm Caribbean Sea.

Water activities: Indulge in a range of water activities, such as snorkelling, scuba diving, kayaking, paddleboarding, and windsurfing.

Beachside Dining: Savour wonderful seafood and tropical beverages at one of the many beachside restaurants and bars.

People-watching: Enjoy the vibrant scene and watch as residents and tourists alike soak up the sun and have fun.

Cost:

Beach entry: Most of Punta Cana Beach is free to enter.

Water Sports: Rental prices for water sports equipment normally vary from $20 to $50 per hour.

Beachfront Dining: Prices for food and drinks at beachfront restaurants vary, but you should expect to pay roughly $10-$20 per meal.

How to Get There:

To access Punta Cana Beach, you can:
Pre-book a private transfer: A handy and hassle-free option, with fees ranging from $25 to USD 100 per vehicle, one-way.

Shared Shuttle: A more budget-friendly option, with rates of about $15-USD 25 per person, one-way.

Taxi: A flexible alternative, but be sure to discuss the fare beforehand. The cost might range from $30 to USD 100, depending on the distance.

Rental Car: Offers maximum flexibility to explore the area. Car rental fees vary but expect to pay roughly $30-$50 USD each day.

Macao Beach
Macao Beach, or Playa Macao, is a gorgeous public beach located on the northeastern coast of the Dominican Republic. Known for its immaculate white sands, crystal-clear turquoise

waters, and big waves, it's a favourite among surfers and adventure seekers.

Scan the QR code

1. Open Camera: Launch your smartphone's camera app.
2. Position QR Code: Place the QR code within the camera's viewfinder.
3. Hold Steady: Keep the device steady for the camera to focus.
4. Wait for Scan: Wait for the code to be recognized.
5. Tap Notification: Follow the prompt to access the content.

Things to Do:

Surfing: Macao Beach is recognized for its superb surfing conditions, with consistent waves throughout the year. Whether you're a seasoned surfer or a beginner, you'll find waves to suit your ability level.

Sunbathing and Swimming: Relax on the smooth beach, soak up the sun, and take a refreshing plunge in the clear waters.

People-watching: Enjoy the dynamic environment and watch as residents and tourists alike enjoy the beach.

Off-Road Adventures: Rent an ATV or buggy and enjoy the magnificent coastal sceneries.

Cost:

Beach Access: Free

Surfboard Rental: Approximately $20-$30 per day

ATV or Buggy Rental: Prices vary, but expect to pay roughly $50-$100 for a half-day rental.

How to Get There:

To access Macao Beach, you can:
Taxi: A taxi is the most convenient method to travel to Macao Beach. The cost will vary based on your starting position.

Rental Car: Renting a car offers the best flexibility to explore the area. You may drive immediately to the beach and explore other surrounding attractions.

Organised Tour: Many tour operators provide day trips to Macao Beach, which include transportation, guided sightseeing, and sometimes lunch.

Remember to carry sunscreen, a hat, and plenty of drink, as the sun can be fierce.

Water Sports

Snorkelling

Snorkelling in Punta Cana
Snorkelling in Punta Cana is an exciting experience, affording a glimpse into the lively underwater world of the Caribbean Sea. With crystal-clear seas and plentiful marine life, the area is a snorkeler's heaven.

Where to Snorkel:
Natural Pools: These hidden natural pools, often formed by coral reefs, provide a tranquil and comfortable environment for snorkelling.

Offshore Reefs: For more experienced snorkelers, offshore reefs offer a broad assortment of marine life, including colourful fish, sea turtles, and coral formations.

Marine Parks: Punta Cana's marine parks offer guided snorkelling tours, providing insights into the local ecosystem and marine conservation efforts.

Cost:

Snorkel Gear Rental: Renting snorkel gear normally costs roughly $10-$20 per person.

Guided Snorkelling trips: Guided trips, which sometimes include equipment rental and transportation, can cost anywhere from $50 to $100 per person.

How to Get There:
To reach the top snorkelling places in Punta Cana, you can:

Book a Snorkeling Tour: Many resorts and tour companies provide guided snorkelling trips, which include transportation, equipment rental, and a knowledgeable guide.

Rent Snorkel Gear: You may rent snorkel gear from several water sports rental establishments around the shore.

Private Boat hire: For a more personalised experience, you can hire a private boat to explore quiet snorkelling sites.
Remember to respect the aquatic environment and avoid touching or harming the coral reefs.

Scuba diving

Scuba Diving in Punta Cana
Punta Cana boasts some of the most magnificent scuba diving destinations in the Caribbean. With crystal-clear seas, vibrant coral reefs, and rich marine life, it's an ideal destination for scuba diving enthusiasts.

Where to Dive:

Catalina Island: This famous dive destination is recognized for its stunning underwater geology, including underwater caves and tunnels.

The Wall: This stunning dive site offers a steep drop-off that plunges into the deep blue, affording breathtaking vistas of marine life.

The Aquarium: This shallow reef is excellent for novices and offers a beautiful display of fish and coral.

Cost:

Certified Diver: A normal two-tank dive, including boat hire, gear rental, and guide expenses, can cost roughly $100-$150.

Certification Course: The cost of a PADI Open Water Diver certification course can range from $300 to $500, depending on the dive centre.

How to Get There:

To reach the dive spots in Punta Cana, you can:

Book a Diving Tour: Many resorts and diving centres provide dive trips that include transportation, equipment rental, and a licensed dive guide.

Lease a Boat: For a more personalised experience, you can lease a private boat to explore certain dive areas.

Important Considerations:

Certification: You must be a qualified diver to engage in scuba diving activities.

Marine Conservation: It's crucial to respect the marine environment and prevent touching or destroying the coral reefs.

Dive Center Selection: Choose a reputable dive centre with competent instructors and well-maintained equipment.

Surfing

Surfing at Punta Cana

While Punta Cana isn't regarded as a world-class surfing destination like Costa Rica or Bali, it nevertheless provides some good surf places, particularly during the winter months. The best waves are often found on the east coast, where the water is more exposed to the swell.

Where to Surf:

Macao Beach: This is the most popular surfing site in Punta Cana, recognized for its big waves and consistent surf.

Playa Blanca: This beach offers a variety of surf breakers, appropriate for both beginners and expert surfers.

Bavaro Beach: While not as renowned for surfing as Macao, Bavaro Beach can produce nice waves, especially during winter months.

Cost:
Surfboard Rental: Renting a surfboard normally costs roughly $20-$30 per day.

Surf instruction: Surf instruction can cost anything from $50 to $100 per hour.

How to Get There:

To reach these surf places, you can:
Cab: A cab is the most convenient way to travel to the surf areas.

Rental Car: Renting a car offers the most flexibility to explore different surf spots and neighbouring areas.

Organized Surf Tour: Many surf schools and tour operators provide guided surf tours, which include transportation, equipment rental, and surf training.

Remember to check the surf forecast before venturing out, as wave conditions might fluctuate based on the season and weather. Additionally, it's crucial to surf responsibly and observe local surf etiquette.

Kiteboarding

Kiteboarding in Punta Cana
Punta Cana offers outstanding conditions for kiteboarding, with constant breezes and warm, clear waters. The area's picturesque beaches and regular trade winds make it a popular destination for kiteboarders of all levels.

Where to Kiteboard:

Kite Beach: This dedicated kiteboarding beach offers great conditions for both beginners and experienced kiteboarders. With its flat water and constant winds, it's great for learning and performing new feats.

Macao Beach: This popular surfing spot also offers superb kiteboarding conditions, especially during the winter months when the waves are higher.

Cost:

Kiteboarding Lesson: A kiteboarding lesson can cost anywhere from $100 to $200, depending on the duration and the instructor's experience.

Kite Gear Rental: Renting kiteboarding gear, including a kite, board, and harness, normally costs roughly $50-$100 per day.

Scan the QR code

1. Open Camera: Launch your smartphone's camera app.
2. Position QR Code: Place the QR code within the camera's viewfinder.
3. Hold Steady: Keep the device steady for the camera to focus.
4. Wait for Scan: Wait for the code to be recognized.
5. Tap Notification: Follow the prompt to access the content.

How to Get There:

To reach the kiteboarding areas in Punta Cana, you can:

Cab: A cab is the most convenient method to travel to the kite sites.

Rental Car: Renting a car offers the most flexibility to explore other kite sites and neighbouring areas.

Organised Kiteboarding Tour: Many kiteboarding schools and tour companies provide guided tours, which include transportation, equipment rental, and instruction.

Remember to check the wind forecast before setting out, since wind conditions can alter during the day. Additionally, it's crucial to kiteboard properly and respect other water users.

Excursions

Island hopping

Island Hopping in Punta Cana

Island hopping in Punta Cana gives a unique opportunity to discover the beautiful splendour of the Dominican Republic's coastline. Several islands, each with its unique appeal, are easily accessible from the mainland.

Popular Island Hopping Destinations:

Saona Island: This pristine island is famed for its immaculate white sand beaches, crystal-clear waters, and diverse marine life. You can sunbathe on the beach, snorkel in the crystal-clear seas, or explore the natural pools.

Catalina Island: This island offers excellent snorkelling and diving opportunities, with beautiful coral reefs and a rich assortment of marine life.

Isla Catalina: This little island is a hidden gem, offering isolated beaches and tranquil waters, great for swimming and snorkelling.

Cost:
The cost of island hopping in Punta Cana varies depending on the chosen trip, the number of islands visited, and the inclusions. Typically, a full-day island hopping excursion, including transportation, lunch, drinks, and activities, can cost anywhere from $50 to $150 per person.

How to Get There:

Coordinated cruises: Most island hopping cruises are coordinated by local tour operators. They offer handy packages that include transportation, guided excursions, and activities.

Private Boat lease: For a more personalised experience, you can lease a private boat to explore the islands at your own speed. This option is excellent for groups of friends or families.

Remember to carry sunscreen, a hat, and plenty of drink, as the sun can be fierce. Additionally, it's crucial to respect the marine environment and avoid destroying the coral reefs.

Dolphin and whale watching.

Dolphin & Whale Watching in Punta Cana

While Punta Cana is mostly known for its magnificent beaches and active nightlife, it also provides great opportunities for dolphin and whale watching.

Dolphin Watching

Dolphin viewing is a popular activity in Punta Cana. Many tour operators provide boat tours that take you out to sea to encounter these lively creatures in their natural habitat. You can regularly observe dolphins swimming beside the boat, leaping out of the water, and performing acrobatic stunts.

Where to go:

Saona Island: This picturesque island is home to a variety of marine life, including dolphins.

Catalina Island: This island also offers opportunities for dolphin watching, especially on boat cruises.

Cost:

The cost of a dolphin-watching excursion normally runs from $50 to $150 per person, depending on the duration of the tour, the size of the boat, and the specific activities included.

How to get there:

Book a Tour: Most dolphin viewing cruises are offered by local tour operators. You can arrange a tour through your hotel or directly with a tour operator.

Whale Watching

Punta Cana is also an excellent spot for whale viewing, particularly during the winter months when humpback whales migrate to the Dominican Republic's warm waters to mate and give birth. While not as frequent as dolphin viewing, whale-watching cruises can be a genuinely remarkable experience.

Where to go:

Samaná Bay: This bay is a renowned whale-watching area, bringing thousands of visitors each year. While it's a bit of a trek from Punta Cana, it's absolutely worth it for the chance to witness these gorgeous creatures.

Cost:
Whale-watching cruises to Samaná Bay normally cost between $150 and $300 per person, depending on the tour operator and the duration of the tour.

How to get there:

Book a Tour: Whale-watching tours to Samaná Bay are normally booked by local tour operators. These tours normally include transportation, a boat cruise, and a skilled guide.

Zip-lining

Zip-lining in Punta Cana
Zip-lining through the lush tropical trees of Punta Cana is an exhilarating adventure that gives amazing views of the surrounding countryside. This thrilling sport allows you to soar through the canopy, feeling the adrenaline rush as you glide from platform to platform.

Where to Zip-Line:

Several adventure parks in Punta Cana provide zip-line courses. Some prominent choices include:

Samaná Bay

Scan the QR code
1. Open Camera: Launch your smartphone's camera app.
2. Position QR Code: Place the QR code within the camera's viewfinder.
3. Hold Steady: Keep the device steady for the camera to focus.
4. Wait for Scan: Wait for the code to be recognized.
5. Tap Notification: Follow the prompt to access the content.

Soles del Caribe Adventure Park: This park offers a variety of adventure sports, including zip-lining, rappelling, and rock climbing.

Monkey rainforest: This park mixes zip-lining with a rainforest excursion, allowing you to encounter rare creatures and birds.

Cost:

The cost of zip-lining in Punta Cana varies depending on the unique park and the length of the course. Generally, you should expect to pay roughly $50-$100 per person for a zip-line trip.

How to Get There:

To reach the zip-line parks, you can:

Book a Tour: Many hotels and tour operators provide zip-line trips, which include transportation, equipment rental, and a guide.

Rent a Car: Renting a car allows the option to explore different adventure parks at your own speed.

Cab: You can also take a cab to the adventure parks, but it may be more expensive than hiring a car or arranging a trip.

ATV tours

ATV Tours in Punta Cana

Embark on an amazing ATV adventure through the Dominican Republic's breathtaking countryside. ATV rides offer an exhilarating opportunity to discover the island's natural splendour, from lush woods to clean beaches.

Where to Go:

Many tour organisations offer ATV trips in Punta Cana. These tours often take you through gorgeous trails, rivers, and plantations.

How to Book:
You may book ATV rides through numerous online platforms and local tour providers. Here are a few prominent websites where you can book ATV trips in Punta Cana:

Viator: This renowned travel website offers a wide choice of ATV trips in Punta Cana. You may compare costs, read reviews, and book your tour online.

Expedia: Another wonderful alternative for arranging ATV trips in Punta Cana. Expedia offers a selection of tour packages, including transportation and guided tours.

Cost:
The cost of an ATV trip in Punta Cana normally runs from $50 to $150 per person, depending on the duration of the tour, the number of stops, and the type of ATV.

How to Get There:
Most ATV tour providers provide transportation from your hotel to the beginning point of the excursion. However, you can also rent an ATV and explore the island freely.

Important Tips:
Wear suitable clothing: Wear comfortable, closed-toe shoes, long pants, and a helmet.
Bring sunscreen and insect repellent: Protect yourself from the sun and pests.

Stay hydrated: Drink plenty of water, especially during the hot, humid days.

Follow the guide's directions: Listen to your guide's instructions and follow all safety standards.

Nightlife

Bars and clubs

Coco Bongo

Coco Bongo is a world-renowned nightclub noted for its high-energy environment, lavish entertainment, and endless cocktails. Located in the centre of Punta Cana, Coco Bongo offers a unique and spectacular nightlife experience.

As soon as you step inside, you'll be immersed in a world of music, dance, and breathtaking performances. The club offers many levels, each with its own bar and dance floor. The main stage features a variety of acts, including acrobatic performances, live music, and celebrity impersonators.

How to Get There:

To travel to Coco Bongo, you can:

Book a Tour: Many hotels and tour companies provide packages that include transportation to and from Coco Bongo.

Taxi: Take a taxi from your hotel to Coco Bongo.

Rental Car: If you have a rental car, you can drive to Coco Bongo. However, it's crucial to realise that drinking and driving is unlawful.

Remember to dress in trendy apparel and get ready for a night of fun and excitement at Coco Bongo.

Mangú
Mangú is a renowned nightclub in Punta Cana, noted for its lively ambiance, energetic music, and entertaining acts. It's a terrific place to dance the night away and experience the exciting nightlife of the Dominican Republic.

How to Get There:

To go to Mangú, you can:
Book a Tour: Many hotels and tour operators provide packages that include transportation to and from Mangú.

Taxi: Take a taxi from your hotel to Mangú.

Rental Car: If you have a rental car, you can drive to Mangú. However, it's crucial to realise that drinking and driving is unlawful.
Remember to dress in trendy attire and get ready for a night of fun and excitement at Mangú.

Imagine Nightclub

Imagine Nightclub is a magnificent and sophisticated nightclub in Punta Cana, giving a unique and amazing nightlife experience. With its modern décor, world-class DJs, and VIP bottle service, Imagine Nightclub is the perfect spot to party the night away.

The club boasts a state-of-the-art music system, amazing lighting effects, and a variety of VIP spaces. Whether you choose to dance the night away or rest in a private booth, Imagine Nightclub has something for everyone.

How to Get There:

To get to Imagine Nightclub, you can:
Book a Tour: Many hotels and tour operators provide packages that include transportation to and from Imagine Nightclub.

Cab: Take a cab from your accommodation to Imagine Nightclub.

Rental Car: If you have a rental car, you can drive to Imagine Nightclub. However, it's crucial to realise that drinking and driving is unlawful.

Remember to dress in elegant apparel and get ready for a night of luxury and excitement at Imagine Nightclub.

Hard Rock Cafe Punta Cana
Hard Rock Cafe Punta Cana is a dynamic and exciting restaurant that offers a unique dining experience blended with rock 'n' roll culture. Located in the heart of Punta Cana, this iconic restaurant and bar is a favourite location for both residents and tourists.

The cafe has a huge dining area and bar, a stage for live music and events, and an outdoor patio excellent for savouring cocktails and people-watching. The menu provides a range of American favourites, such as renowned burgers, hot sandwiches, and fresh salads, all cooked with fresh, high-quality ingredients.

While you enjoy your meal, you can admire the collection of rock 'n' roll memorabilia displayed throughout the cafe. The energetic environment, combined with the wonderful cuisine and drinks, makes Hard Rock Cafe Punta Cana a must-visit location for anybody searching for a fun and unforgettable night out.

How to Get There:

To get to Hard Rock Cafe Punta Cana, you can:

Cab: Take a cab from your hotel or any other area in Punta Cana.

Rental Car: If you have a rental car, you can drive to the Hard Rock Cafe.

Walk or Bike: If you're staying nearby, you can walk or bike to the cafe.

Remember, drinking and driving is forbidden, so please plan your transportation properly.

Chapter 4.Cultural Experiences

Dominican Culture and History

Local Cuisine

Must-try dishes

Mofongo

Mofongo is a Puerto Rican delicacy prepared from fried green plantains, mashed into a dough-like consistency, and typically packed with garlic, pork rinds (chicharrones), and other ingredients. It's often served with a protein, such as shrimp, chicken, or beef, and a flavorful sauce.

Cost:

The cost of a plate of mofongo can vary based on the restaurant and region, however, it normally runs from $10 to USD 20.

Sancocho

Sancocho is a substantial and savory stew that is a staple in many Latin American countries, including the Dominican Republic. It's a slow-cooked stew that often includes a range of meats, such as beef, chicken, and hog, along with root vegetables including yuca, yautia, plantains, and corn. The broth is seasoned with a blend of herbs and spices, resulting in a thick and flavorful soup.

Cost:

The cost of a bowl of sancocho might vary based on the restaurant and area. However, you can normally expect to pay from $8 to USD 15 for a substantial dish.

Arepas

In the Dominican Republic, arepas are a sweet dessert, considerably distinct from the savory maize cakes found in other Latin American countries. They're a deep, delicious cake prepared with cornmeal, milk, sugar, and spices like cinnamon. They're commonly served with a cup of coffee for breakfast or as a dessert.

Cost:

The cost of an arepa in the Dominican Republic can vary based on the locale, but they're normally quite reasonable, ranging from $1 to USD 3.

Tostones

Tostones are a famous Dominican side dish made from green plantains. They're fried twice, giving in a crispy and delicious delicacy. Tostones are commonly eaten with a variety of foods, including stews, meats, and shellfish.

Cost:

The cost of a side order of tostones at a restaurant in the Dominican Republic normally ranges from $2 to USD 5.

Street food

Empanadas

Empanadas are a popular street snack in the Dominican Republic. They consist of a fried or baked pastry filled with a savory filling, generally made with ground beef, chicken, or cheese. They are a delightful and pleasant snack or dinner.

Cost:

The cost of an empanada in the Dominican Republic varies depending on the area and the filling. Generally, you may anticipate paying between $1 to $3 USD for each empanada.

Yaniqueques

Yaniqueques are a wonderful Dominican street dish, frequently similar to North American Johnny Cakes. These savoury, deep-fried flatbreads are produced using a simple dough of wheat, water, salt, and sometimes butter or oil. They can be consumed simply, with a sprinkle of salt, or filled with cheese, meat, or veggies. Yaniqueques are a popular snack or breakfast meal in the Dominican Republic, frequently served with a cup of coffee or hot chocolate.

Cost:

Yaniqueques are normally fairly economical, costing roughly $1-2 USD each piece.

Ceviche

Ceviche is a famous Latin American meal made with fresh raw fish cured in citrus juices, generally lime or lemon. In the Dominican Republic, it's generally made with white fish like tilapia or grouper, and it's seasoned with lime juice, onions, cilantro, and sometimes chilli peppers. The acidity of the citrus juice "cooks" the fish, giving it a delicate and acidic flavour.

Cost:

The cost of ceviche in the Dominican Republic might vary based on the restaurant and region. However, it's often an economical dish, with prices ranging from $8 to USD 15.

Churros

Churros are a famous fried dough delicacy, commonly enjoyed as a snack or dessert. They're often long, thin strips of dough that are deep-fried till golden brown and crispy on the exterior, while soft and fluffy on the inside. Churros are often served with a side of chocolate sauce or caramel for dipping.

Cost:

The pricing of churros might vary based on the region and vendor. However, they are often a pretty reasonable treat, with prices ranging from $1 to $3 USD.

Local drinks

Mamajuana

Mamajuana is a distinctive and strong alcoholic beverage from the Dominican Republic. It's produced by infusing a mixture of rum, red wine, and honey with a blend of tree bark and herbs. The final combination is a black, rich drink with a somewhat bitter taste and a tinge of sweetness.

While the specific recipe varies, the base ingredients often include:

- **Rum**: Usually a dark rum

- **Red Wine**: A dry red wine

- **Honey**: A natural sweetener

Tree Bark and Herbs: A mix of native herbs and tree bark, which give the drink its characteristic flavour and reputed medical benefits.

Mamajuana is often aged for several months or even years to achieve its full flavour. It's considered to provide several health benefits, including boosting the immune system and increasing sexual health.

Cost:
The cost of marijuana might vary depending on the brand, size, and where you acquire it. Generally, you should anticipate paying anywhere from $20 to USD 50 for a bottle.

Piña Colada
A Piña Colada is a tropical beverage made with pineapple juice, coconut cream or milk, and rum. It's a sweet, creamy, and refreshing drink that's excellent for sipping on a hot day. The cocktail is generally served with a pineapple wedge or a cherry.

Cost:
The cost of a Piña Colada might vary based on the region and the institution. In a beach bar or resort in the Dominican Republic, you can expect to pay around $10-15 USD for a cocktail.

Batida de Coco
Batida de Coco is a delicious and creamy coconut cocktail, popular in the Dominican Republic and other tropical countries. It's created with coconut milk, condensed milk,

and a spirit like cachaça or vodka. The drink is often served with coconut flakes or a cherry.

Cost:
The cost of a Batida de Coco might vary depending on the locale and the specific bar or restaurant. However, it's often a budget-friendly drink, costing roughly $5-USD 10.

Morir Soñando
Morir Soñando, which translates to "To Die Dreaming," is a pleasant and popular Dominican drink. It's a simple yet tasty concoction of orange juice and milk, often sweetened with sugar and flavoured with vanilla. The drink is normally served cold and is ideal for soothing thirst on a hot day.

Cost:
As a frequent and affordable drink, Morir Soñando is usually quite inexpensive. You may anticipate paying roughly $1 to USD 3 for a glass, depending on the region and the business.

Chapter 5. Sample Itineraries

Short Weekend Getaway

A Short Weekend Getaway in Punta Cana

A Perfect 3-Day Escape

Punta Cana offers the perfect escape for a quick weekend break. With its magnificent beaches, colourful culture, and exquisite cuisine, you can pack a lot into a few days. Here's a sample itinerary for a 3-day trip:

Day 1: Arrival and Beach Bliss

Morning: Arrive at Punta Cana International Airport and proceed to your accommodation. Check-in and relax by the pool or beach.

Afternoon: Explore the gorgeous beaches of Bávaro or Punta Cana. Rent a jet ski, go for a swim, or simply relax on the sand.

Evening: Enjoy a great supper at a beachfront restaurant, followed by a night out at a local bar or nightclub.

Day 2: Adventure and Culture

Morning: Embark on an adventure tour, such as zip-lining through the rainforest or visiting the natural pools.

Afternoon: Visit a local market to explore the vivid culture and purchase souvenirs.

Evening: Enjoy a romantic supper at a beachfront restaurant, followed by a leisurely evening stroll along the beach.

Day 3: Island Hopping and Farewell

Morning: Set off on a boat cruise to Saona Island or Catalina Island. Spend the day swimming, snorkelling, and sunbathing on the gorgeous beaches.

Afternoon: Return to the mainland and relax by the pool or beach.

Evening: Pack your bags and transfer to the airport for your departure.

Tips for a Perfect Weekend Getaway:

Book in Advance: To assure availability, especially during peak season, book your flights and accommodations in advance.

Pack Light: Pack only the necessities to minimise baggage costs and make your journey more convenient.

Protect Your Skin: Apply sunscreen regularly to protect your skin from the powerful Caribbean sun.

Stay Hydrated: Drink plenty of water to stay hydrated, especially in the hot and humid atmosphere.

Learn a Few Spanish Phrases: Knowing a few basic Spanish phrases can enrich your travel experience and help you connect with the people.

One-Week Vacation

A One-Week Paradise: Your Punta Cana Itinerary
A week in Punta Cana is the perfect amount of time to relax, explore, and make lifelong memories. Here's a sample itinerary to help you make the most of your vacation:

Days 1-3: Beach Bliss and Water Adventures

Day 1: Arrive in Punta Cana and check into your hotel. Spend the rest of the day lounging by the pool or beach, enjoying the magnificent views and crystal-clear waters.

Day 2: Embark on a spectacular water excursion. Choose from a choice of sports such as snorkelling, scuba diving, or parasailing. Explore the beautiful undersea world, see marine creatures, or soar above the ocean.

Day 3: Take a boat ride to Saona Island or Catalina Island. These lovely islands provide pristine beaches, crystal-clear waters, and chances for swimming, snorkelling, and sunbathing.

Days 4-5: Cultural Exploration and Nightlife

Day 4: Visit a local market to explore the vivid culture and purchase souvenirs. You can also take a guided tour to learn about the history and culture of the Dominican Republic. In the evening, enjoy a fantastic dinner at a local restaurant and delight in the active nightlife.

Day 5: Take a day trip to Santo Domingo, the capital of the Dominican Republic. Explore the old Colonial Zone, visit the Alcázar de Colón, and observe the spectacular architecture.

Days 6-7: Relaxation and Farewell

Day 6: Spend a relaxed day at the pool or beach, reading a book, sipping on a beverage, or simply enjoying the tranquillity.

Day 7: Pack your bags and check out of your hotel. Transfer to the airport for your departure flight, cherishing the memories of your fantastic week in Punta Cana.

Chapter 6.Practical Tips

Safety Tips

Safety Tips for Your Punta Cana Vacation
While Punta Cana is generally a safe destination, it's always wise to take steps to ensure a hassle-free trip. Here are some safety guidelines to keep in mind:

Personal Safety

Stay mindful: Be mindful of your surroundings, especially in crowded situations.
Valuables: Keep your valuables protected in a hotel safe. Avoid carrying significant quantities of cash.

Nighttime Safety: If you're going out at night, stay in well-lit places and use recognized transportation.

Respect Local Customs: Dress modestly, especially while visiting religious places or local communities.

Water Safety

Ocean Currents: Be careful of ocean currents and rip tides, especially when swimming.
Water Sports: If you're participating in water sports, ensure you're adequately trained and equipped.

Sun Protection: Protect yourself from the sun by wearing sunscreen, a hat, and sunglasses.

Health and Wellness

Drink Bottled Water: To avoid waterborne infections, drink only bottled water.

Food Safety: Choose recognized restaurants and avoid street food that may not be hygienic.

Insect Repellent: Use insect repellent to protect yourself from mosquito bites, especially during the rainy season.

Medical Insurance: Ensure you have appropriate travel insurance to handle any medical emergency.

Getting Around

Taxi

Taxis in Punta Cana
Taxis in Punta Cana are a convenient method to get around, especially if you're staying at a resort and want to explore the local area.

Routes:
Taxis can take you to different destinations inside Punta Cana, including:

Beaches: Bávaro Beach, Punta Cana Beach, Macao Beach

Shopping Centers: Palma Real Shopping Village, Downtown Punta Cana

Local Attractions: Scape Park, Hoyo Azul Cenote

Restaurants and Bars: Various local and foreign dining alternatives

Terminals:

Taxis can be available at:
Punta Cana International Airport: Taxis are widely accessible at the airport, and you can negotiate a fee with the driver.

Hotels and Resorts: Many hotels and resorts have taxi stands where you can arrange transportation.

Downtown Areas: Taxis can be hailed on the street or obtained at taxi stands.

Cost:
It's vital to understand that taxis in Punta Cana are not metered. You'll need to arrange the fare with the driver before commencing your trip. The cost can vary depending on the route, time of day, and traffic conditions. It's wise to negotiate a fair fee before getting into the taxi.

Rental Car

Renting a Car in Punta Cana
Renting a car in Punta Cana offers the utmost flexibility to explore the island at your speed. You can quickly move between different beaches, attractions, and towns.

Routes:
Punta Cana International Airport to Bávaro: This is a popular route for beachgoers and resort-hoppers.

Punta Cana International Airport to Punta Cana: This route takes you to the main town area, where you can find stores, restaurants, and nightlife.

Punta Cana International Airport to Macao Beach: This path goes to a wonderful, less populated beach with big waves, great for surfing.

Punta Cana to Santo Domingo: A lengthier drive, but offers the opportunity to explore the Dominican Republic's capital city.

Terminals:

Rental automobile Companies: Several international and local automobile rental companies operate at Punta Cana International Airport.

Cost:
Automobile rental fees vary depending on the rental business, automobile type, and rental term. On average, anticipate to pay roughly $30-USD 50 every day.

Public Transportation (Bus)
While public transit options in Punta Cana are limited compared to other large cities, here's an overview of what's available:

Public Buses (Guaguas):
Routes: Local buses, called "guaguas," connect several sites within Punta Cana, including famous tourist areas like Bávaro and Punta Cana.

Terminals: Bus stops are located throughout the city.

Cost: Fares are relatively modest, averaging under 1 USD for short trips.

Intercity Buses:

Routes: Intercity buses connect Punta Cana to other major cities in the Dominican Republic, such as Santo Domingo.

Terminals: Major bus terminals can be found in bigger cities.

Cost: Fares vary based on the distance, but normally range from 5 to 10 USD.

Walking

Walking in Punta Cana
While Punta Cana is predominantly a resort destination, walking can be a delightful method to explore some regions, especially within resort complexes and town centres.

Routes:

Resort Grounds: Many resorts have well-maintained sidewalks and paths, making it easy to roam around the site and enjoy the amenities.

Beachfront Promenade: The beachfront promenade in some regions offers a lovely walking path along the coast.

Downtown Areas: In places like Punta Cana Village, you may walk to shops, restaurants, and bars.

Biking

Biking in Punta Cana
Biking in Punta Cana offers a unique way to discover the gorgeous scenery and colorful culture of the region. While there aren't specific bike pathways throughout the city, many resorts and villages inside Punta Cana offer well-maintained bike paths and trails.

Routes:
Resort Bike Lanes: Many resorts in Punta Cana have their bike lanes, great for leisurely rides and enjoying the resort's attractions.

Coastal Roads: Some coastal roads offer scenic paths for riding, allowing you to enjoy ocean vistas and fresh air.

Off-Road paths: For more ambitious riders, there are off-road paths through the lush tropical forests and along the shoreline.

Terminals:
Bike Rentals: Many resorts and local businesses provide bike rentals, allowing you to explore at your own pace.

Cost:
Bike rental rates might vary depending on the rental time and type of bike. Generally, you should expect to pay roughly $15-$30 per day for a standard bike rental.

Important Considerations:

Road Safety: Be cautious when biking on roadways, as traffic conditions might be unpredictable.

Heat & Humidity: Be careful of the hot and humid atmosphere, especially throughout the day.

Hydration: Stay hydrated by drinking plenty of water.

Sun Protection: Wear sunscreen, a hat, and sunglasses to protect yourself from the sun.

While riding can be a fun and eco-friendly way to explore Punta Cana, it's vital to plan your routes carefully and prioritize safety.

Packing Essentials

Packing Essentials for Your Punta Cana Trip
Packing the correct stuff for your Punta Cana trip can make a great difference in your comfort and enjoyment. Here's a checklist of crucial points to consider:

Clothing:

Swimwear: Bring several swimsuits for beach days and aquatic activities.

Lightweight apparel: Pack lightweight, breathable apparel, such as shorts, t-shirts, and sundresses.

Cover-ups: Bring cover-ups to wear over your swimsuit.

Hat and Sunglasses: Protect yourself from the sun with a wide-brimmed hat and sunglasses.

Evening Wear: If you plan on dining at fancy restaurants or heading to nightclubs, pack some dressier apparel.

Footwear:
Flip-Flops: Essential for beach days and poolside relaxing.

Water Shoes: Protect your feet from pebbles and coral whether snorkelling or visiting the beach.

Comfortable Walking Shoes: For exploring the town or going on excursions.

Toiletries:

Sunscreen: High-SPF sunscreen is needed to protect your skin from the powerful Caribbean sun.

Insect Repellent: Protect yourself from insect bites, especially during the rainy season.

After-Sun Lotion: Soothe your skin after sun exposure.

Basic Toiletries: Pack travel-sized toiletries to conserve space.

Documents:

Passport: Ensure your passport is valid for at least six months beyond your travel dates.

Visa: Check the visa requirements for your nationality.

Travel Insurance: It's essential to get travel insurance to cover any unexpected medical crises or trip cancellations.

Booking Confirmation: Keep your flight, hotel, and tour confirmations accessible.

Electronics:

Camera: Capture your moments with a nice camera or smartphone.

Charger: Don't forget to pack a charger for your equipment.

Power Adapter: If necessary, bring a power adapter to accommodate different electrical outlets.

Additional Tips:

Pack Light: Pack light to save baggage costs and make your journey more convenient.

Roll Your garments: Rolling your garments can assist conserve space in your suitcase.

Use Packing Cubes: Packing cubes can help you organise your luggage properly.

Check Baggage Restrictions: Be mindful of your airline's baggage restrictions.

Health and Wellness

Health & Wellness Tips for Your Punta Cana Vacation

To guarantee a healthy and pleasurable trip to Punta Cana, consider the following health and wellness tips:

Hydration

Drink Plenty of Water: The tropical climate can be dehydrating. Drink plenty of water throughout the day to stay hydrated.

Avoid Excessive Alcohol Consumption: While it's tempting to indulge in tropical cocktails, drink wisely and keep hydrated.

Sun Protection

Wear Sunscreen: Apply broad-spectrum sunscreen with a high SPF to protect your skin from damaging UV radiation.

Wear a Hat and Sunglasses: Shield your face, eyes, and head from the sun.

Food Safety

Choose Reputable Restaurants: Opt for restaurants with appropriate cleanliness practices.

Avoid Street Food: While tempting, it's recommended to avoid street food, as it may not be as hygienic.

Wash Fruits and Vegetables: If you're eating fresh produce, wash it properly to eradicate any bacteria.

Insect Protection

Use Insect Repellent: Apply insect repellent to protect yourself from mosquitoes, especially during the rainy season.

Wear Long Sleeves and Pants: In the evening, wear long sleeves and pants to minimise exposure to mosquitoes.

Medical Precautions

Travel Insurance: Purchase adequate travel insurance to cover any medical problems.

Consult a Doctor: Consult your doctor before your travel to discuss any necessary vaccines or prescriptions.

Pack Essential prescriptions: Bring any prescription prescriptions you may need.

Chapter 7. Conclusion

Final thoughts and recommendations

Final Thoughts and Recommendations

Punta Cana offers a genuinely memorable experience, with its pristine beaches, colourful culture, and kind hospitality. As you plan your trip, remember to mix rest and activity to develop a personalised agenda.

Final Thoughts:

Embrace the Local Culture: Immerse yourself in the Dominican culture by trying local cuisine, listening to live music, and socialising with the friendly locals.

Respect the Environment: Be attentive to the environment and prevent littering. Respect marine life and coral reefs, especially when snorkelling or diving.

Savour the Moment: Take time to absorb the beauty of the beaches, the crystal-clear waters, and the energetic atmosphere of Punta Cana.

Recommendations:

Book in Advance: Especially during peak season, it's wise to book your flights, hotels, and tours in advance.

Pack Light: Pack only the necessities to minimise baggage costs and make your journey more convenient.

Protect Yourself from the Sun: Use sunscreen, and wear a hat, and sunglasses to protect your skin from the powerful Caribbean sun.

Stay Hydrated: Drink plenty of water to stay hydrated, especially in the hot and humid atmosphere.

Consider All-Inclusive Resorts: All-inclusive resorts offer convenience and value, with food, drinks, and activities included in the fee.

Learn simple Spanish Phrases: Knowing a few simple Spanish phrases can enrich your travel experience and help you connect with the people.

Travel Insurance: Invest in comprehensive travel insurance to protect yourself against unexpected catastrophes.
With careful planning and a good mindset, your trip to Punta Cana will be an amazing experience.

Where to go next in the Dominican Republic

After witnessing the beauty and excitement of Punta Cana, you might wish to explore other places in the Dominican Republic. Here are a few suggestions:

Santo Domingo:

Historical Charm: Immerse yourself in the rich history of the Dominican Republic by visiting the Colonial City, a UNESCO World Heritage Site.

Cultural Exploration: Explore the Ozama fortification, the first fortification built by Europeans in the New World, and the Alcázar de Colón, the former palace of Christopher Columbus's son.

Vibrant City Life: Experience the busy city life, savour delicious Dominican food, and shop at local markets.

Samaná Peninsula:

Whale Watching: Witness the awe-inspiring phenomenon of humpback whales migrating to the warm waters of the Dominican Republic.

Water Adventures: Enjoy water activities like kayaking, snorkelling, and diving in the crystal-clear waters.

El Limón Waterfall: Hike through thick jungles to reach this gorgeous waterfall and take a refreshing swim.

Puerto Plata:

Amber Museum: Explore the fascinating world of amber and learn about the Dominican Republic's rich past.

Fort San Felipe: Visit this 16th-century fortress and enjoy magnificent views of the city and the ocean.

Cable Car journey: Take a cable car journey up to Pico Isabel de Torres for stunning views of the surrounding area.

Las Terrenas:

Relaxing Beaches: Enjoy the gorgeous beaches and crystal-clear waters of Las Terrenas.

Water Sports: Engage in a range of water sports, such as windsurfing, kitesurfing, and sailing.

Nightlife: Experience the active nightlife with a variety of pubs, restaurants, and clubs.

By touring these sites, you can explore the various beauty and cultural diversity of the Dominican Republic.

Useful Websites and Contact Information for Travelers to the Dominican Republic

Official Tourism Website

GoDominicanRepublic.com: This is the official tourism website for the Dominican Republic. It gives detailed information on places, activities, lodgings, and travel suggestions.

Government Resources

U.S. Department of State: This website provides travel advice and information for U.S. citizens travelling to the Dominican Republic.

- **Website**:
  https://travel.state.gov/content/travel/en/internatio nal-travel/International-Travel-Country-Information-Pages/DominicanRepublic.html

- **Emergency Number**: +(809) 567-7775

Airlines

- **American Airlines**: Major airline serving the Dominican Republic.

- **Delta Air Lines**: Major airline serving the Dominican Republic.

- **United Airlines**: Major airline serving the Dominican Republic.

- **Southwest Airlines**: Budget airline serving the Dominican Republic.

Car Rental Companies

- **Avis**: Offers automobile rental services in the Dominican Republic.

- **Budget**: Budget automobile rental services in the Dominican Republic.

- **Hertz**: Hertz automobile rental services in the Dominican Republic.

Accommodation Booking Websites

- **Booking.com**: A prominent website for booking hotels and accommodations.

- **Expedia**: Another popular website for booking hotels and accommodations.

- **Airbnb**: A platform for booking holiday rentals.

Local Tour Operators

- **Viator**: Offers a choice of excursions and activities in the Dominican Republic.

- **Expedia**: Provides a wide selection of tour alternatives, including island hopping, adventure trips, and cultural experiences.

Emergency Numbers

- **Police**: 911

- **Fire Department**: 911

- **Ambulance**: 911

Remember to check for any updates or changes to travel advisories and rules before your journey.

Safe Travels!

Common and Useful Phrases for Interacting with Locals in the Dominican Republic

Here are some simple Spanish words that will help you navigate your way across the Dominican Republic:

Basic Greetings and Farewells

- Hola: Hello

- Buenos días: Good morning

- Buenas tardes: Good afternoon

- Buenas noches: Good evening/night

- ¿Cómo estás? How are you?

- Estoy bien, gracias: I'm well, thank you.

- Gracias: Thank you

- De nada: You're welcome

- Adiós: Goodbye

Essential Phrases for Travelers

- ¿Dónde está el baño? Where is the bathroom?

- ¿Cuánto cuesta? How much does it cost?

- ¿Habla inglés? Do you speak English?

- Por favour: Please

- Gracias: Thank you

- Lo siento: I'm sorry

- ¿Puedes ayudarme? Can you help me?

- Necesito un cab: I need a taxi

Common Phrases for Ordering Food and Drinks

- Quiero comer: I want to eat

- Quiero beber: I want to drink

- ¿Qué me recomiendas? What do you recommend?

- La cuenta, por favor: Check, please

Cultural Tips

Dominicans are polite and welcoming: Don't hesitate to strike up a discussion with locals.

Learn a few basic Spanish words: Even a few simple sentences can go a long way in demonstrating respect and appreciation.

Be patient and understanding: Communication barriers may develop, so be patient and attempt to speak clearly.

Embrace the local culture: Immerse yourself in the local culture by sampling the food, listening to the music, and engaging in local events.

Here's a draft of an emotionally compelling message to readers:

Your Journey to Paradise Starts Here

As you go on your voyage to the magnificent sands of Punta Cana, I hope this book acts as your valued friend. I've poured my heart and soul into producing every page, pulling from my personal experiences and significant research.

Your favourable evaluations and opinions are vital to me. They not only validate my efforts but also inspire me to continue publishing high-quality travel guides. By expressing your thoughts, you're not just assisting me but also future travellers who will benefit from your observations.

I've devoted substantial time and energy to exploring Punta Cana's hidden beauties, sampling its wonderful cuisine, and experiencing its vibrant culture. My goal is to give you all the important information to make your trip unforgettable.

So, when you browse through the pages of this guide, let it transport you to the sun-kissed beaches, lush jungles, and pulsating nightlife of Punta Cana. And when you return from your trip, please share your experiences and feedback. Your words will help me continue to deliver the finest possible travel advice.

Made in the USA
Columbia, SC
03 January 2025

50966967R00046